W9-CDO-205

AR. 0.5

EXPLORING DINOSAURS

IGUANODON

By Susan H. Gray

THE CHILD'S WORLD®
CHANHASSEN, MINNESOTA

Published in the United States of America by The Child's World®
PO Box 326, Chanhassen, MN 55317-0326
800-599-READ
www.childsworld.com

Photo Credits: American Museum of Natural History: 15; Corbis: 5 (A & J Verkaik),
7, 13 (Philip James Corwin); Douglas Henderson: 6, 22, 24, 27; Getty Images/Hulton
Archive: 18; Michael Skrepnick: 10; Mike Fredericks: 11-top and bottom, 17; Photo
Researchers/Mehau Kulyk: 21; Photo Researchers/Science Photo Library: 14, 25 (Chris
Butler); Royal Belgian Institute of Natural Sciences/Thierry Hubin: 19; Todd Marshall:
9, 12 (Lisa Marshall), 23.

The Child's World®: Mary Berendes, Publishing Director

Editorial Directions, Inc.: E. Russell Primm, Editorial Director; Ruth M. Martin, Line
Editor; Katie Marsico, Assistant Editor; Matthew Messbarger, Editorial Assistant; Susan
Hindman, Copy Editor; Susan Ashley, Proofreader; Tim Griffin, Indexer; Kerry Reid,
Fact Checker; Cian Loughlin O'Day, Photo Reseacher; Linda S. Koutris, Photo Selector

Original cover art by Todd Marshall

The Design Lab: Kathleen Petelinsek, Design and Art Direction; Kari Thornborough,
Page Production

Library of Congress Cataloging-in-Publication Data
Gray, Susan Heinrichs.
  Iguanodon / by Susan H. Gray.
     p. cm. — (Exploring dinosaurs)
Includes index.
Contents: Watch your step—What is an Iguanodon?—Who found the first
Iguanodon?—What did Iguanodon do every day?—Where did Iguanodon live?
  ISBN 1-59296-187-8 (lib. bdg. : alk. paper)
  1. Iguanodon—Juvenile literature. [1. Iguanodon. 2. Dinosaurs.] I. Title. II. Series.
QE862.O65G7455 2004
567.914—dc22   2003018626

Content Adviser:
Peter Makovicky,
Ph.D., Curator,
Field Museum,
Chicago, Illinois

TABLE OF CONTENTS

CHAPTER ONE

WATCH YOUR STEP!

A thunderstorm was moving in. Dark clouds rolled across the sky. The air smelled damp and musty. **Cycad** branches waved and rattled as the wind picked up. Lightning flickered in the distance. Then silence. Suddenly, a thunderclap shook the forest.

Iguanodon (ig-WAH-nuh-don) awoke with a start. She looked around. Other members of the herd lifted their heads and blinked sleepily. Some stretched their necks and yawned. A few peered across the landscape, looking for possible dangers. A second thunderclap brought them all to their feet. Every one—large or small— knew it was time to get out of there. The herd began moving away from the sound of the thunder.

Much like the storms of today, storms in prehistoric times were both helpful and destructive. They provided water for plants and animals, but they also sometimes caused fires and floods.

Iguanodon probably traveled in herds. Scientists believe several different kinds of dinosaurs did this as a means of protection, with adults walking on the outside and younger animals staying on the inside for safety.

Soon they broke into a trot. Pounding across the land, they trampled all the plants in their path. They crushed ferns and flattened bushes. Little furry creatures skittered out of the way.

Suddenly, the lead dinosaur vanished! Then the five right behind him disappeared as well. Six more—zip! Then all the rest—gone! Every single dinosaur in the herd had run right off the edge of a steep

ravine. As they slid down, they struggled wildly. Arms and legs flailed. Tails thrashed. Hands grabbed at thin air.

The dinosaurs fell hundreds of feet before they landed at the bottom of the ravine. Unable to move, they lay in a heap. The sky darkened as the storm moved overhead. Lightning lit up the whole ravine. Thunder boomed every few minutes. And rain fell on the heap of unlucky animals all evening and into the night.

It's also possible that the Iguanodon herd ran off the edge of the ravine after being frightened by meat-eating dinosaurs searching for a meal. Whether it was thunder or the presence of predators, the fall killed more than 30 Iguanodon.

CHAPTER TWO

WHAT IS AN IGUANODON?

An *Iguanodon* is a dinosaur that lived from about 132 million to 100 million years ago. Its name is taken from the Spanish word *iguana* (ig-WAH-nuh) and the Latin word for tooth. An iguana is a large lizard that eats plants. Its teeth have ridges. *Iguanodon*'s teeth look a lot like those of an iguana, only much larger.

From the tip of its snout to the end of its tail, *Iguanodon* was about 33 feet (10 meters) long. When it rose up on its back legs, it stood 16 feet (5 m) tall. The dinosaur probably weighed between 4 and 5 tons.

Iguanodon's back legs were thick and heavy. Each foot had three toes, and each toe ended in a thick, unsharpened claw.

Iguanodon had teeth that measured about 2 inches (5 centimeters) long and a hinged upper jaw that was able to move from side to side. Unlike many other dinosaurs, it chewed its food instead of swallowing it whole.

The **reptile** had arms that were much smaller than its legs. It could bend over and use its arms for walking, or rear up and walk on two legs.

The dinosaur's hands were quite unusual. The three middle fingers were grouped together and shared a fleshy pad. The little

Scientists originally thought Iguanodon *walked on two legs and stood hunched over like a kangaroo. They now know the dinosaur spent most of its time on all fours and stood on its hind legs mostly to run or reach tall plant matter.*

fingers were very flexible and could fold inward to help the hands grasp and hold. The *Iguanodon's* thumbs were no more than thick spikes. They stood apart from the rest of the fingers and pointed inward. An *Iguanodon* with its hand in the air probably looked like it was giving a thumbs-up sign!

The animal's heavy head ended in a short, round mouth. It had a bony beak, much like a turtle's, in the front of its mouth. Many teeth filled its cheeks and jaws. The dinosaur's neck was broad and its body was wide. *Iguanodon*'s thick tail was almost as long as the rest of its body. The dinosaur probably lifted its tail off the ground to travel.

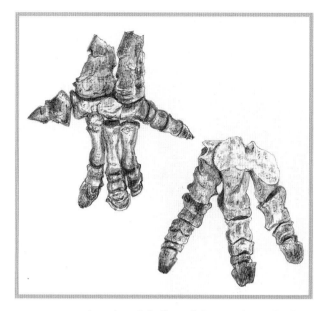

An Iguanodon *hand (left) and foot (right). The feet were similar to hooves, and the spike-like thumbs on the hands were probably useful for gathering food and defending against predators.*

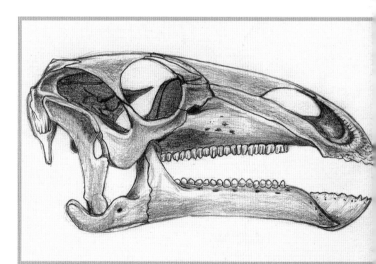

Iguanodon*'s strong beak allowed the dinosaur to eat a variety of plant matter. Twigs and tougher plants could wear the beak down over time, but it was constantly growing and therefore managed to stay sharp.*

WHAT COLOR WAS *IGUANODON?*

Scientists seem to know a lot about this dinosaur. They know about its odd hands, its teeth, and its tail. What can they tell us about *Iguanodon*'s color?

Scientists can only guess about the color of the dinosaurs. A few pieces of skin and skin imprints have been found on rocks. But most dinosaur skin just rots away. Even if a piece survives, it's colorless— its **pigments** have broken down or washed away long ago.

Still, paintings today show dinosaurs in all kinds of colors. *Iguanodon*, for example, appears as a brown, gray, or green animal. Sometimes it is shown with spots or stripes. Sometimes its skin looks blotchy. Artists don't just dream up these colors and patterns. They often talk to scientists before they paint.

Scientists can tell them that many of today's

reptiles are brown, gray, or green. They also know that reptiles often have very bright colors. Some turtles, for example, have orange spots on their heads. Some snakeskins are colored with deep shades of gold, red, and black. Other reptiles have patterns, stripes, or spots.

Modern animals have different skin colors for different reasons. Dark colors help them absorb heat. Bright colors help them scare enemies away. Striped or spotted skin can help with camouflage. Dinosaur skin probably had the same uses millions of years ago. So artists show them in all sorts of colors. We'll probably never know exactly what color *Iguanodon* was. But we can make some pretty good guesses.

CHAPTER THREE

WHO FOUND THE FIRST *IGUANODON?*

The first *Iguanodon* **fossils** were found by either Gideon Mantell or his wife, Mary Ann. Gideon was a British doctor in the 1800s. Like other doctors of his day, he had many interests. He especially liked to study rocks and animals. Mary Ann often helped him with his work.

According to one story, the two were out in their carriage on a spring day. Gideon was visiting

Many people say that Mary Ann Mantell was the first person to discover an Iguanodon *fossil. The tooth she found is currently on display at a national museum in Wellington, New Zealand.*

a patient, and Mary Ann was along for the ride. During the trip, Mary Ann spotted some oddly shaped fossils by the side of the road. She picked them up and showed them to her husband. Neither one knew what the fossils were from. So they brought them back home to show others.

Gideon Mantell made important contributions to dinosaur paleontology, but he didn't have an easy life. His hobby of collecting and studying fossils proved expensive, and he became so desperate that he turned his home in Brighton, England, into a public museum. The museum ultimately failed, but Mantell continued writing about reptile fossils until his death in 1852.

Gideon took the fossils to many experts, but no one could figure out what they were. He even showed them to paleontologists

(PAY-lee-un-TAWL-uh-jists). These are people who study fossils of **ancient** plants and animals. Finally, one person realized these were the teeth of some unknown creature. In fact, he said, they looked a lot like the teeth of an iguana.

This took place in the 1820s. At that time, scientists knew about fossils. But they didn't know about dinosaurs. Although a few dinosaur bones had been discovered, no one had quite figured out what they were. Most people thought they were bones of giant elephants, rhinoceroses, or even humans! The idea that the bones came from giant reptiles was beyond belief.

Gideon Mantell wrote articles telling about the *Iguanodon* fossils. He thought the animal was some sort of lizard that grew 60 feet (18 m) long. He believed it had a little horn on its nose.

In time, scientists realized that *Iguanodon* was not a lizard

at all. In fact, it became one of the first animals to be called

a dinosaur.

A cartoon showing Gideon Mantell thinking about Iguanodon. *In his efforts to identify the fossils his wife had discovered, Mantell studied an iguana tooth at the Hunterian Museum in Glasgow, Scotland. After this visit, he determined that his fossils belonged to a prehistoric animal that was simply a much larger version of the modern-day iguana.*

AN INCREDIBLE FIND

The year was 1878. Coal miners in Belgium were gathering for another day of work. They buttoned up their jackets and lit their lanterns. Then they descended into the blackness of the mine. Down they went, for more than a thousand feet. Daylight disappeared behind them and their eyes slowly adapted to the darkness.

Suddenly, one miner saw something. It was an old tree trunk filled with gold! He and his friends raced toward it and began digging at the precious metal. But soon their hearts sank. They realized it was only fool's gold. The shiny material was worthless.

As it turned out, the tree trunk was the real treasure. Word got out about the strange trunk, and other people came to see it. In time, someone recognized it as a big *Iguanodon* bone. Scientists came to check it out. They inspected the

floor and walls of the mine. They peered into cracks and crevices. All of their searching paid off. Deep in the mine, they discovered the skeletons of about 30 *Iguanodons*.

The work didn't stop there! The bones had to be chipped from the rock and hauled from the mine. They had to be cleaned and put together. Many of the skeletons were pieced together in a church—the only place big enough for the job.

Scientists figured that the dinosaurs had slipped down a ravine and died. They rested deep in the earth for millions of years. Today, the *Iguanodons* have a new home. The herd is in a museum in Belgium for everyone to see.

CHAPTER FOUR

What Did *Iguanodon* Do Every Day?

Iguanodon probably spent most of its time just eating and sleeping. The dinosaur was a plant eater, or herbivore (UR-buh-vore). When it was hungry, it used its hard, toothless beak to tear off pieces of plants. It ripped up cycads and tore branches from **conifers.** Its rows and rows of cheek teeth ground the material down. Paleontologists think that for *Iguanodon* to keep its weight steady, it would have had to eat hundreds of pounds of food every week.

When the dinosaur stooped down, it could eat low-growing ferns. When it stood up on its hind legs, it could reach leaves and branches that were 16 feet (5 m) above the ground! A herd of *Iguanodons* may have stripped an area clean, then moved on.

Museum visitors studying an Iguanodon *skeleton in the late 1800s. Although* Iguanodon *spent most of its time on all fours, it could travel at relatively quick speeds on its hind legs, as well. By studying fossilized footprints and analyzing a dinosaur's weight and the length of its legs, scientists can estimate how fast the animal was able to move.*

An *Iguanodon* in a hurry probably rose up on its back legs and ran. Some paleontologists believe the dinosaur trotted at about 9 to 12 miles (15 to 20 kilometers) an hour. That's about the speed of a bicycle rider.

The dinosaur was probably not a fierce fighter. It did not have sharp teeth. Its body was not covered with heavy plates. It did not

Traveling in a herd was one way for Iguanodon *to defend itself against meat-eating predators.*

A mother Iguanodon *with her babies. Herds were also a good way to protect younger* Iguanodon, *since some meat-eating dinosaurs would deliberately attack animals that seemed small or weak.*

have horns on its head or spikes on its tail. Instead, *Iguanodon*

protected itself in other ways. It lived in a herd, where members

could look out for each other. Some could warn others of danger.

Large dinosaurs could shield smaller ones. And if attacked,

Iguanodon could always use its thumb spikes.

CHAPTER FIVE

WHERE DID
IGUANODON LIVE?

guanodon roamed many lands. The dinosaur lived during a

stretch of time called the Cretaceous (kreh-TAY-shuss) period.

During this time, the Earth was very different from the way it is

today. Back then, the continents were packed more closely together.

A wide variety of dinosaurs existed during the Cretaceous period. At the end of this period, many prehistoric species—including all the dinosaurs—underwent a huge mass extinction. Scientists believe this may have been caused by an asteroid hitting the Earth, changes in climate, or volcanic eruptions.

Africa and South America were right next to each other. Europe and North America were not very far apart.

Over millions of years, the continents drifted apart. In fact, the continents are still moving around today. Scientists tell us they move between 0.4 and 4 inches (1 and 10 centimeters) every year.

The Earth experienced continental drift about 100 million years ago. German scientist Alfred Wegener thought that a supercontinent existed before continental drift occurred. Wegener named this supercontinent Pangaea, *which means "all land" in Greek.*

Today, the continents are spread out. Animals cannot always walk from one continent to the next. But when the continents were close together, animals might have easily been able to do this. *Iguanodon* walked the Earth for more than 20 million years.

Perhaps, at a certain point, it traveled from Europe to North America. Maybe it was able to go back and forth between Africa and Asia.

Iguanodon skeletons have been found in Europe, Africa, North America, and Asia. These dinosaurs might have been able to live in so many places because they had such an easy time getting there. They didn't have to swim mighty oceans to reach new continents. They just had to keep walking.

Unfortunately, some of them walked right off the edge of a ravine one day! About 10 million years after they disappeared, *Iguanodon* became extinct. That was about 100 million years ago. It wasn't until 1878 that some coal miners in Belgium made an incredible discovery. Surely, more *Iguanodons* are just waiting to be found. Maybe you'll be the next to find one!

Although many questions remain about Iguanodon, *this dinosaur has had a major impact on paleontology. After* Iguanodon *fossils were first discovered nearly 200 years ago, scientists began to consider the possibility that giant, prehistoric reptiles once roamed the Earth. Paleontologists have built upon this knowledge and continue to solve the mysteries surrounding dinosaurs and the world in which they lived.*

Glossary

ancient (AYN-shunt) Something that is ancient is very old; from millions of years ago. Paleontology is the study of ancient plant and animal life.

camouflage (KAM-uh-flaj) Camouflage is a way for animals, people, and objects to blend in with their surroundings. Sometimes an animal's skin color is good camouflage.

conifers (KON-eh-furz) Conifers are plants that have cones. The hungry *Iguanodon* fed on conifers.

cycad (SY-kad) A cycad is a palmlike tree with tough branches and leaves. When *Iguanodon* was hungry, it dined on cycads.

fossils (FOSS-uhlz) Fossils are the remains of ancient plants or animals. Fossils teach us about the things that lived millions of years ago.

pigments (PIG-munts) Pigments are what give skin its color. An *Iguanodon*'s color would depend on what pigments it had in its skin.

ravine (ruh-VEEN) A ravine is a narrow valley with steep sides. The *Iguanodon* skeletons found in Belgium were probably from a herd that fell into a ravine.

reptile (REP-tile) A reptile is an air-breathing animal with a backbone and is usually covered with scales or plates. *Iguanodon* was a reptile.

Did You Know?

▶ An early drawing by Gideon Mantell showed *Iguanodon* with a horn on its nose. Mantell had found one thumb spike among the dinosaur's bones. He thought it belonged on the animal's nose. Not until much later did scientists realize this was completely wrong.

▶ *Iguanodon* footprints have been found on an island near England. The footprints clearly show that the animal had three toes.

▶ At least one *Iguanodon* skull is in such good shape that it shows where the dinosaur's head muscles and blood vessels were.

The Geologic Time Scale

TRIASSIC PERIOD

Date: 248 million to 208 million years ago

Fossils: *Coelophysis, Cynodont, Desmatosuchus, Eoraptor, Gerrothorax, Peteinosaurus, Placerias, Plateosaurus, Postosuchus, Procompsognathus, Riojasaurus, Saltopus, Teratosaurus, Thecodontosaurus*

Distinguishing Features: For the most part, the climate in the Triassic period was hot and dry. The first true mammals appeared during this period, as well as turtles, frogs, salamanders, and lizards. Corals could also be found in oceans at this time, although large reefs such as the ones we have today did not yet exist. Evergreen trees made up much of the plant life.

JURASSIC PERIOD

Date: 208 million to 144 million years ago

Fossils: *Allosaurus, Anchisaurus, Apatosaurus, Barosaurus, Brachiosaurus, Ceratosaurus, Compsognathus, Cryptoclidus, Dilophosaurus, Diplodocus, Eustreptospondylus, Hybodus, Janenschia, Kentrosaurus, Liopleurodon, Megalosaurus, Opthalmosaurus, Rhamphorhynchus, Saurolophus, Segisaurus, Seismosaurus, Stegosaurus, Supersaurus, Syntarsus, Ultrasaurus, Vulcanodon, Xiaosaurus*

Distinguishing Features: The climate of the Jurassic period was warm and moist. The first birds appeared during this period. Plant life was also greener and more widespread. Sharks began swimming in Earth's oceans. Although dinosaurs didn't even exist at the beginning of the Triassic period, they ruled Earth by Jurassic times. There was a minor mass extinction toward the end of the Jurassic period.

CRETACEOUS PERIOD

Date: 144 million to 65 million years ago

Fossils: *Acrocanthosaurus, Alamosaurus, Albertosaurus, Anatotitan, Ankylosaurus, Argentinosaurus, Bagaceratops, Baryonyx, Carcharodontosaurus, Carnotaurus, Centrosaurus, Chasmosaurus, Corythosaurus, Didelphodon, Edmontonia, Edmontosaurus, Gallimimus, Gigantosaurus, Hadrosaurus, Hypsilophodon, Iguanodon, Kronosaurus, Lambeosaurus, Leaellynasaura, Maiasaura, Megaraptor, Muttaburrasaurus, Nodosaurus, Ornithocheirus, Oviraptor, Pachycephalosaurus, Panoplosaurus, Parasaurolophus, Pentaceratops, Polacanthus, Protoceratops, Psittacosaurus, Quaesitosaurus, Saltasaurus, Sarcosuchus, Saurolophus, Sauropelta, Saurornithoides, Segnosaurus, Spinosaurus, Stegoceras, Stygimoloch, Styracosaurus, Tapejara, Tarbosaurus, Therizinosaurus, Thescelosaurus, Torosaurus, Trachodon, Triceratops, Troodon, Tyrannosaurus rex, Utahraptor, Velociraptor*

Distinguishing Features: The climate of the Cretaceous period was fairly mild. Flowering plants first appeared in this period, and many modern plants developed. With flowering plants came a greater diversity of insect life. Birds further developed into two types: flying and flightless. A wider variety of mammals also existed. At the end of this period came a great mass extinction that wiped out the dinosaurs, along with several other groups of animals.

How to Learn More

At the Library

Lambert, David, Darren Naish, and Liz Wyse. *Dinosaur Encyclopedia.*
New York: DK Publishing, 2001.

On the Web

Visit our home page for lots of links about *Iguanodon:*

http://www.childsworld.com/links.html

Note to Parents, Teachers, and Librarians: We routinely verify our
Web links to make sure they're safe, active sites—so encourage
your readers to check them out!

Places to Visit or Contact

AMERICAN MUSEUM OF NATURAL HISTORY
*To view numerous dinosaur fossils, as well
as the fossils of several ancient mammals*
Central Park West at 79th Street
New York, NY 10024-5192
212/769-5100

CARNEGIE MUSEUM OF NATURAL HISTORY
*To view a variety of dinosaur skeletons, as well as fossils related
to other reptiles, amphibians, and fish that are now extinct*
4400 Forbes Avenue
Pittsburgh, PA 15213
412/622-3131

DINOSAUR NATIONAL MONUMENT
To see several dinosaur fossils
11625 East 1500 South (Quarry)
Jensen, UT 84035
435/781-7700
or
4545 E. Highway 40
Dinosaur, CO 81610-9724
Bozeman, MT 59717-2730
406/994-2251 or 406/994-DINO (3466)

MUSEUM OF THE ROCKIES
To see real dinosaur fossils, as well as robotic replicas
Montana State University
600 West Kagy Boulevard
Bozeman, MT 59717-2730
406/994-2251 or 406/994-DINO (3466)

NATIONAL MUSEUM OF NATURAL HISTORY
(SMITHSONIAN INSTITUTION)
To see several dinosaur exhibits and special behind-the-scenes tours
10th Street and Constitution Avenue, N.W.
Washington, D.C. 20560-0166
202/357-2700

Index

About the Author

Susan H. Gray has bachelor's and master's degrees in zoology, and has taught college-level courses in biology. She first fell in love with fossil hunting while studying paleontology in college. In her 25 years as an author, she has written many articles for scientists and researchers, and many science books for children. Susan enjoys gardening, traveling, and playing the piano. She and her husband, Michael, live in Cabot, Arkansas.